Poems from

the

Flat Earth

Written by H.G. Maguire

Copyright

Visit www.youtube.com/johndoylepoems for audio recordings of the poems by the Author. For more information : email johndoylepoems@gmail.com

Published in the United Kingdom by H.G.Maguire

DEDICATION

For my wife Anikie,

for my children Michelle, Aleena and Ayden

my dad, mum and sister,

those who helped and inspired and all who support.

Contents

Care!

You say you don't care about the shape of the earth

That it doesn't matter if it's flat or a ball,

But what about the lies we are told

Can you just go by your day without a care,

What about the children needlessly dying of

Diseases that we cured in shores far away

What about the waste of man's life

Manufacturing the same objects with different names,

Does none of this matter to you,

What about the innocent born children

That grow up and end in the streets

Because they didn't collect the leaves from the trees

What about all that is around you

And the way we live,

Don't you think it could be better done

Where you work to survive

Only one life to be a factory skivvy,

And that's all you were born to do,

Don't you care about all the money that others have

And keep in the bank,

And print when they need but not for you

Living five in a one bedroom flat,

Don't you care about any of this,

That what you're taught is just that,

Programmed and put in line

To never be you,

Don't you care about any of this,

No, yes,

Must be no,

Because we are all still living the same way,

No improvement

In the way we all suffer day by day,

In this existence that was shaped after creation

To keep us all in the same places,

And our selfish species

Not caring about truths

Covering our eyes with deception

And living another mans hell.

You are the love of eternal dreams

As the days dwindle and become shorter

I feel the love between us

My heart still sings the same song

Never wanting to be apart

Always together

Lying next to you till the end.

You are the love of eternal dreams

Rising my soul to the highest heights

I will love you, till our last breath of this earth

And our souls entwine the ether becoming one

Living forever.

How does it feel to be free

How does it feel to be free?

To be that one per cent

That can do all they please

With no monetary worries

Will no plans or expectations

To work or not work

The choice is yours

To do whatever is your passion

To not need to be told

You can or can not do

Or are not qualified enough

But with money buy you way in

Or create your own dream

How does it feel to be free?

Are those that believe they are free

Because they are told they are

But do not realise their mind is captive

To the thoughts before them

Building an illusion of freedom

For being free is not just liberty

Not just seeing no walls or wires

But being able to do as you please

To live your life as if your dream

To pursue all you wish

To have no barrier for this one shot existence

Freedom should be complete

Not limited,

How does it feel to be free,

And those than can tell

Why do you keep it to yourself!

'we are just shaven caveman in a suit'

We are just shaven cavemen in a suit

Pretending to be something we are not

Inventing words to describe away

That we do not really know,

Living our lives with an air of assumption

Believing to be civilised and intelligent

Never to be challenged or reversed

Follow, repeat and do.

We are just shaven cavemen in a suit

Always repeating the same mistakes.

The trial of mankind (in the pursuit of truth)

Where is it I stand, this plain, this earth, this realm,

Is it the trial of mankind which we all undertake

Where each eye sees its own reflection

In the pursuit of truth.

Peaceful revolution

How would we achieve a peaceful revolution of this
existence?
When the problem with humans is usually to make
change, they make war
Change is hardest thing, not only the change within
But the one we have lesser power over; the change
around us,
But when we awake, we will understand together,
We always had the power, we just gave it away!

The world is not as it seems, the lies have covered
your eyes
You, blinded by the flashing lights of the tv set
Need to awake and think for yourself
And explore the world you inhabit,
And find true, the truth around you
That was always there, yet you did not know.

We need to achieve a peaceful revolution of this
existence
Awake, think, stand, seize the power and make the
change
Bring this light of truth to all and live in peace as was
intended.

In the silence

in the silence,

we seek the hope of truth,

and its reign over us all,

so that all can live as born equally.

'who wrote my mind'

Who wrote my mind?

Why do I think what I think?

Do what I do,

Enjoy what I like

And hate what I do not,

Who wrote the script?

The code, the web, the thoughts

Hidden within my synapse?

Can I rewire my brain?

Change my thoughts,

Correct parts I no longer want or like

Why is it so hard to change?

To stop a feeling or a thought that you don't like

When starting it was so easy.

Over time was I conditioned?

Did I choose,

Have I forgot a seconds choice

That have led me to where I am now,

How do I not know where my thoughts and feelings

Emotions and passions come from,

Am I answerable for what I am,

Did I create me, or was I created?

The Painter

I am a painter, who with oils and colours

Expresses the hidden view which we all see

As I stand at my easel, I am unable to

Stroke onto the canvas my view

For I have come to understand the truth

For I was born like any other

And through my long life

I was taught all that I now know,

Very little came from my own endeavour

And most of my foundation of my way

Was brought to me when I was but a child

Now I am grown

And I look through eyes that have been shaped

Like how I shape the colours on a canvas

To express a feeling to you,

But it is a creation, a construct of sorts

And now I see my life too is the same,

My parents were my painters

They took my blank canvas of a life

And brought colour and oils to it

As did teachers, and friends and authorities

And then I was complete a finished masterpiece

Able to live on, but through the way I was painted,

But now I see, the hidden drawings

The sketches, the lines, the strokes,

The colours merged over to cover up mistakes,

I see the lies,

The lies of my existence,

I am but a man,

Who was shaped like every other,

We all started off like me a blank canvas

And now we follow in the way we were taught

But I with my own mind

Even though it has been shaped

I can think independent thoughts of a sort

Whether I can truly say they are mine

I am not sure,

Not that I am insane or mad

But that I have been taught how to see, how to think,

Even how to feel,

By so many when I was a babe,

But these thoughts I have,

Have shown me my existence too is a painting

That has been painted,

A construct,

Not a reality as such,

For I see in front of me a tree,

But it is not a tree

What it is I know not,

Nobody does, save God if he does exist

For we found all this like babies

And gave names to all around

And all accepted this

And made up words and meanings

To all that is around us,

But how do I now forget

Forget as a painter I am

Construct views and feelings everyday

That what I am and what I see

Is but a mere painting

I am an observer, a viewer

Like a man in a museum seeing my painting

But we are within this living painting

And are living paintings ourselves.

I wonder to myself,

Can I then like a painter,

Change what I see in front of me,

And yes, for that tree, I can call another name

And so it is,

As long as we all agree,

And the suffering that I have painted

Of children crying as those they love die

Of diseases long since cured

Can I change this,

But the problem is, I am merely a painting within a painting

And I have not the brushes or instruments

To change these things,

But I call out to you all

That you must awake and see

The painting within the painting

And understand the meaning of such

And begin the changes

Need to make mankind a masterpiece

Of true beauty of which it can be!

Failings

I created the chaos

The moment that led

To my own destruction

Without thinking

I acted and that was the end

If i could go back

And take control of the reins

I would but sadly that is not possible

We are all tied inextricably

To every moment

That we experience but once

And often have no time

To act as we would wish

Yet we will all too often

Forget and imprison

Those that fall fail of the same

Failings.

Prison

I was born from a prison, contained,

To a four walled prison, a home,

I went to many prisons, schools,

I drove around in my prison, a car,

I had many jobs in prisons, offices,

I bought food in a prison, shopping centres,

I was buried in a prison, my coffin,

Into the ground, my final prison,

Whilst all along in the prison, the Earth!

We were born prisoners, lived as prisoners

And died as prisoners

Believing ourselves free.

I am a child

I am a child

I was born into a world

Of injustice and inequality

I look around me

At those older and see them

Doing nothing about it

I see them smiling and enjoying

Passing the time

They do nothing to change the system

They teach me their same bad ways

And worst of all their truthful lies

All hoping i will swallow

And will never question it all.

I am a child

Who expected better from you all

You have continued to let us all down

Those born and to be born

Because you are all content

With the way the world is

Yet i do hear your moans and cries

But nothing is done,

You say you have no power

But you are all the power there is.

I am a child

Who wishes he wasn't born

Because the world you give me

Is full of lies, injustice, death, disease,

Poverty, inequality,

But you will still ignore me

And cover it up with more truthful lies,

Though in your heart of hearts

Deep down you know what i say isn't wrong!

I'm beaten

I'm beaten, I give up, I surrender

I have tried to fight for justice, equality, freedom,

To attain what other's have and I should have

But you win, your system with its illogical ways

Has tied up every avenue I tried to go down,

I can't keep banging my head of the walls your built

For our existence,

The world we have no choice but to live

The pain that I am receiving

I can't take it anymore,

I have to let go,

Let you win

Stay where you want me,

Without.

Everything is about money, proving your money

Getting on ladders, which are impossible for you to,

You help those with money even when you say you

help us,

I see through your lies,

When you will help us pay rent but not mortgage

So we always pay those with money, who need no

help

But never help us get out of this situation,

You make us take term life insurance, as if we know

when we'd die,

You make us fill out form after form,

With the names we were given,

Go around and around through your hopes

Divided, divided species,

We must stay within our borders

Must fight against one another,

Must be distracted by all around us,

So we continue to live this existence, this system,

Never fighting to change it

For a better one,

Where we are all equal and free,

Yet we are told we have this already

But are you free, is everyone equal and okay,

Are you blind or stupid,

If you think you have those things

People are dying of curable conditions,

Of starvation, having to live a waged life,

Buying leasehold houses over and over again,

Taking possession of land and things which are not

yours,

Come on, wake up, wake up,

Truly look at every person around you,

And those you cannot see or feel

And ask yourself, do you only care if you and yours are

okay,

But we are all one species

That have been divided by man made words and

concepts

Do you want us to always be this way

For some to suffer and some not,

Don't you think we could find a way

Without all these resources and minds

So that every single living person could be happy,

You'll say its impossible

Because that's how you've been taught to think,

Get past your programming

And see the truth,

The truth that we are able to do all we want,

Or we can live the stories that had been passed down,

You know we have free will and power

All of us exactly the same,

No one has more than another,

The stories of bosses, celebrities, is just that stories,

No one stands above another,

We are all truly equally born,

It's the stories that create illusions,

So are you deceiving yourself through your only life,

And we are living in pain and misery

For what reason,

Wake up, think, make the change!

I was born without a name

I was born without a name,

My name was given to me,

My education was given to me

My world was given to me,

I was taught to want, to own possessions

Through birthdays and Christmas,

I was taught to vote from only two people

I was taught I was free and lived in democracy

whilst neither of these were true

I was told I was coloured and was given a myth of

ancestry

But I was never told we were all one species

No different from one another, all born with a clean

slate

And all taught through our place and time

Everything around us

From eyes that saw before us.

Our World

Our World is full of lies and deceit,

Injustices,

Inequalities,

layer after layer,

but opening our eyes and minds

against the system we have been taught

is the most difficult task that

we all must undertake,

in order to live in truth and harmony.

I used to be

I used to be scared, used to fear

Then it all changed

I feel like a different man

Though i know i am the same

What changed, what wised me up

Was it watching my wife give birth

To my twins, her courage , their beauty

Learning the truths of the world

Question everything, false flags, flat earth

Those youtubers empowered me

By reinforcing my knowledge

Of the fake world, existence we live in

The inequality, the injustices.

I used to bow to other man

Thinking they greater than me

But we are all the same

And the rest is illusion

Divisions of cast, creed, race

All set us up against one another

So we don't stand up for ourself

Respecting baa baa black sheep's master

Now i see the bullshit more than i ever did

I am truly as free as can be in this slave system

But it's not enough

Now i need you all to awake

To see the monopoly rules you live in

To tear them up and reinvent humanity

Into a better order, a system that serves all

Not those with riches and power

Born with silver spoon,

To truly be free to inhabit this place

And its fruits with need of paying twice

To what was freely given

To strive for humanity

Not continuing some other man's dream.

'Of souls united living within a dream'

I don't wanna dream, see the places I've never been

Too long have we walked with our eyes shut

Whilst the lonely children scream and cry

I don't want to pass another day on this dreary world

It's been long enough travelling the river of misery

The ever-flowing sacrificial tears

Of souls united living within a dream,

I don't want to walk around eyes wide open asleep

Want to make the change, that in dreams are free

Make this world a better place, the one its meant to

be

With no borders or divisions, no falsehoods or misery

With justice and happiness,

I want this world now,

Before I die, before my child grow with the same old

lies

Don't you want the same thing too?

Get Tae Fuck (for Des allison/ YT Sheeps N Neeps)

Get tae fuck

The globe, false flags

Get tae fuck

All the lies

All the lies

Get tae fuck

All the politicians governing us

Get tae fuck

All the inequalities,

the injustices

Get tae fuck

All the suffering

All the diseases

Get tae fuck

All the businesses making money out of misery

Get tae fuck

All the people propping up this world

Get tae fuck

All those sheep with their eyes closed

Get tae fuck

All those keeping the truth from the people

Get tae fuck

All those medicines not curing us

Get tae fuck

All the deception, the borders dividing us

Get tae fuck

All sophistry,

the spinning stories,

The fallacies

36

Get tae fuck

Those with power and control

Who allow this world to continue

Get tae fuck

All of us; who with equal power

Let this all happen

Get tea fuck friday

Open your eyes

Breathe in

Begin.

Scared

Scared, scared of what they'll say

What have they found

What do they know

Why do they make us wait

Worrying over every possibility

Why can't they tell us now

So we can start the fight

The fight of our life

Why must we live in constant fear

Of what may await around every corner

Times master plan unfolding

Genie not going back in bottle,

Help us, fear not, no matter what

And enjoy what is to come.

Apart from you (dedicated to my love, Anikie Annah Maguire)

I don't want to live alone

Apart from you,

You are all i ever wanted

All i ever dreamed

You complete my life

I am unable to be

Without you by my side.

I don't want to wake

And find you gone

Never to return

I'd rather be gone too

In hope of finding you.

My heart longs for you,

Are souls are entwined

Our love unique, special

Like a rainbow in the sky.

I love you, i always will

No one else

Has or could replace you

Or compete,

You made my life

You took my heart, soul, life

And raised it so high,

You made me complete, happy,

Loved.

If the choice was made

You wake up, you wear the clothes you were given,

You eat the food that was prepared for you,

You read the news they tell you,

You live your life by the way you were taught,

To walk down streets you do not own,

You show your tree paper passport

To leave one bit of land to another

Each attached by a name by a man long dead,

You pay tree paper money to make your way,

You possess people and things at work,

Youve been told how to dream, how to see,

You see the caged zoo animals that you think you

know their names

You walk in the world thinking you

Know all you see,

You see a spinning globe in infinite space

And think you know where you live,

You see apes and think you know where you came,

You see books high up, you think you know why you

are here,

But all of it is simply not true,

Possibly part truth, whole lot of lies,

You were like everyone else born

And with your own eyes you should

Have discovered the world

But you were, before you could make choice

Programmed, taught, schooled

How to live,

And what you can know and

You still follow the tracks where you were led

Rather than jump off and see everything

Through your own eyes

And make sense of how it all really should,

Could be

If the choice was made!

All I've ever done

All I've ever done

Was done to survive

You can judge me on one moment

If you chose

But that's like picking one chapter of a book and

reading no further

You don't see what led upto it

Or what may follow

But you'll do it just the same

Everyday

We are all human

We all make mistakes and bad choices

Of varying degrees

We were all born with no manual

And into a system we had no choosing

Remember all this next time

You judge another fellow human being!

If i were dead

If i were dead these would be

My words to you,

I miss you and love you,

I enjoyed all the people i knew and loved,

It was the best experience,

I was lucky to taste of if

I hope i appreciated it,

The only negative was how life was lived

The greed, the money, the waste,

The business of slave life,

The injustices and inequalities

All the children dying needlessly

Because of man's selfish choices

To live the way we did

And any part i played in it,

But i am free now and you too will be

We all will be, maybe it will show us

How better to be where we all go to,

I love you my darling wife and children

Don't Mourne me, for we had each other

And that was the important thing,

The rest is illusion,

Love you then and now.

Once, me, you

Once the time has been found

There's no taking it back again

Never to be rewound, repeated,

Its gone, just a memory slowly fading

As time continues to move on

Without me, without you.

We, the deluded people

We, the deluded people

Who live lies believing truth

Who impose false beliefs from the past

With eye closed to the inequality caused

And the ongoing suffering to those

Who see now the truth of existence

That we born one, indivisible from one another,

brother , sister

With a one chance existence

To experience the natural beauty of life

Yet those men of the caves polluted

The freedom given and constructed

A world, a system, that would delude

Future born into believing they had everything

When they had nothing at all.

What it must be like to be truly free?

What it must be like to be truly free

With no inhibitions or structures

Holding you back,

To live your life as you choose

To not be afraid of those

Who would put you down

Or judge you by your actions

Or impulses

Who would look at you

Through their trained eyes

Their tied-up brains

Believing your can't be this or can't do that

Because of this or that

But who made up the rules,

The straight jacket we clothe ourselves in,

Is it for our betterment or to make us alike,

Who all be prisoners of restriction

In this once off life?

They die by day; they die by night

They die by day; they die by night

Innocent children in a war-torn country

With their eyes fresh they look to the world

Without understanding imbued

To why one man would want to kill another

In order to make pavement of the land

As if it was his to own and yet was freely found.

They die by day; they die by night

Screaming woman told their husband daddy is gone

His life cut short by a piece of metal found

In his eyes before he died

He remembered the sweet smell of life

His wife close by him, his children with a hug

The sun rising across the horizon

All that beauty was given away by a gun in his hand.

They die by day; they die by night

Wars break out, people run,

Explosions ring out, buildings crumble

Blood runs down, sticky and warm

Lake, rivers, oceans of blood

Till the last drop is gone.

They die by day; they die by night

In a world we once found ourselves free

Chained we became

Till our minds were filled

With all the ways we had to live

And breed it did; the inhumanity in humanity

That we would take arms to kill our brethren

In order for power, position, fame, money, land

All illusionary aspects of our kingdoms.

We die by day; We die by Night

Living a past we should have long evolved

Caging our minds in stories of old

When will man out step to his future

And all reclaim the beauty of existence!